A New
Lamp-Lighter
Book

When glowing lamps confront the night,
Then darkness must give way to light.
Thus many a legend, brought to view,
Confirms the Bible's truth anew.

Rays of Historical Truth from the Neglected Scriptures of Ancient Times

Portents

of the

Coming

Millennium

Portents

of the

Coming

Millennium

Dudley F. Cates

Pentland Press, Inc.
England • USA • Scotland

PUBLISHED BY PENTLAND PRESS, INC.
5122 Bur Oak Circle, Raleigh, North Carolina 27612
United States of America
(919)782-0281

ISBN: 1-57197-107-6
Library of Congress Catalog Card Number 98-065629

Printed in the United States of America

To ALEX

Who awaits our arrival, with wings,

safely in his Father's mansion.

Other books by the author:

The Rise and Fall of King Nimrod (1998)
Blossoms of The Nile (1999)

THE DEATH OF ABEL

And it came to pass . . . Cain rose up against his brother, and slew him. And the Lord said unto Cain, Where is Abel thy brother? And he said, I know not: Am I my brother's keeper? . . . (Genesis 4: 8,9)

THE DELUGE

And every living substance was destroyed which was upon the face of the ground, both man, and cattle, and the creeping things, and the fowl of the heaven; and they were destroyed from earth: and Noah only remained alive, and they that were with him in the ark . . . (Genesis 7:23)

THE DOVE SENT FORTH FROM THE ARK

And the dove came in to him in the evening; and lo, in her mouth was an olive leaf pluckt off; so Noah knew that the waters were abated from off the earth . . . (Genesis 8:11)

THE FLIGHT OF LOT

Then the Lord rained upon Sodom and Gomorrah brimstone and fire from the Lord out of heaven . . . his [Lot's] wife looked back from behind him, and she became a pillar of salt . . . (Genesis 19:24,26)

PART ONE

What Really Happened in the Days of Noah

The Full Story of
Why God Destroyed Noah's World
By a Year-long Deluge

Prologue

As the second millennium of the Christian dispensation nears its end, and with the start of a new millennium only a few months away, many people across the world wonder how, if, and when the present age is scheduled by God to draw to its close—to be followed by events graphically described by God's prophets in the Old Testament and by His Son in the New Testament. The revelation of future events, with a cryptic but veiled description of them, is the message to Christians from God Himself, as revealed to His Son and passed on to us through His messenger (angel) to John, "the beloved disciple," on the Island of Patmos about the year A.D. 96. Those who look for signs of the times must ask themselves whether any such signs can be seen on the near horizon, or whether the modern world is simply continuing to move along an unplanned course toward an unpredictable future.

In Matthew 24:36, Christ told His disciples: "But of that day and hour no one knows, not even the angels of heaven, nor the Son, but the Father only. As were the days of Noah, so will be the coming of the Son of Man."

It is not overly presumptuous to note that He made no mention of the other time elements—weeks, months, or years. In fact, He adjured them moments later to: "<u>Watch</u>, therefore, for you do not know on what <u>day</u> your Lord is coming—for the Son of Man is coming at an <u>hour</u> you do not expect." Again He warns them: "<u>Watch</u>, therefore, for you know neither the <u>day</u> nor the <u>hour</u>" (Matthew 25:13).

This book is designed to acquaint Christians, and others who may be sufficiently curious, with some of the signs which were foretold to signal the end of the age. It does so by describing the sordid and depraved conditions of life both before the flood, and again before the destruction of Sodom, as revealed in the historical and non-canonical scriptures which graphically describe these conditions.

We should not be discouraged from attempting to search for the year, or even the month, of this inevitable, extraordinary event. In the words of King Soloman, the wisest man who ever lived, "It is the glory of God to conceal things, but the glory of Kings is to search things out."

Finis

The Days Of Noah

Foremost among the prophetic warnings given by Jesus Christ to His disciples concerning His future return to earth are two which compare events of that predicted time with documented events of the past. In Matthew 24:37-39, He told them:

"As were the days of Noah, so will be the coming of the Son of Man. For as in those days before the flood they were eating and drinking, marrying and giving in marriage, until the day when Noah entered the ark, and the flood came and swept them all away, so will be the coming of the Son of Man."

In Luke 17:26-30, Christ repeated this ominous warning and added the second warning, as He again addressed His disciples:

"As it was in the days of Noah, so will it be in the days of the Son of Man. They ate, they drank, they married, they were given in marriage, until the day when Noah entered the ark, and the flood came and destroyed them all. Likewise, as it was in the days of Lot—they ate, they drank, they bought, they sold, they planted, they built, but on the day when Lot went out from Sodom, fire and sulphur rained from heaven and destroyed them all—so it will be on the day when the Son of Man is revealed."

The severity of these warnings could scarcely be greater, since they were pronounced on a future generation by the Lord himself. If Christians of today tend to ignore them, it may be due, at least in part, to our ignorance of the true conditions of life in each of the times named. Without a fuller understanding of those conditions, it is difficult to draw parallels or make actual comparisons with our lives and societies today.

Very little is revealed in the Old Testament by which we can fully appreciate the depths of wickedness to which our antediluvian ancestors had sunk by the time of Noah. A brief hint of those conditions appears in Genesis 6:5-8, which states that:

"The Lord saw that the wickedness of man was great in the earth, and that every imagination of the thoughts of his heart was only evil continually. And the Lord was sorry that He had made man on the earth, and it grieved him to his heart. So the Lord said, 'I will blot out man whom I have created from the face of the ground, man and beast and creeping things and birds of the air, for I am sorry that I have made them.' But Noah found favor in the eyes of the Lord."

Forceful rhetoric, indeed, but Scripture is rather short on facts about the specific forms of wickedness prevalent in those times. Some of the latter is discussed by the eminent Jewish historian Flavius Josephus, writing (in A.D. 90-95) the history of his forebears (*Antiquities of the Jews*, Book One, Chapters 2 and 3).

Following is Flavius Josephus' brief record of the gradual degradation of society which occurred among Adam's descendants up to the time of the deluge:

"Adam and Eve had two sons. The elder of them was named Cain, which name, when it is interpreted, signifies a possession; the younger was Abel, which signifies sorrow. They had also daughters. Now, the two brethren were pleased with different courses of life; for Abel, the younger, was a lover of righteousness, and, believing that God was present at all his actions, he excelled in virtue, and his employment was that of a shepherd. But Cain was not only very wicked in other respects, but was wholly intent upon getting, and he first contrived to plough the ground. He slew his brother on the occasion following; they had resolved to sacrifice to God. Now Cain brought the fruits of the earth, and of his husbandry; but Abel brought milk, and the first fruits of his flocks. But God was more delighted with the latter oblation, when he was honored with what grew naturally of its own accord, than he was with what was the invention of a covetous man, and gotten by forcing the ground. Whence it was that Cain was very angry that Abel was preferred by God before him; and he slew his brother and hid his dead body, thinking to escape discovery. But God, knowing what had been done, came to Cain, and asked him what was become of his brother, because he had not seen him (for) many days, whereas he used to observe them conversing together at other times. But Cain was in doubt with himself, and knew not what answer to give to God. At first he said that he was himself at a loss about his brother's disappearing; but when he was provoked by God, who pressed him vehemently, as resolving to know what the matter was, he replied he was not his brother's guardian or keeper, nor was he an observer of what he did. But in return, God convicted Cain as having been the murderer of this brother and said, "I wonder at thee, that thou knowest not what is become of a man whom thou thyself hast destroyed." God therefore did not inflict the punishment [of death] upon him, on account of his offering sacrifice, and thereby making supplication to him not to be extreme in his wrath to him; but he made him accursed, and threatened his posterity in(to) the seventh generation. He also cast him, together with his wife, out of that land. And when he was afraid that in wandering about he should fall among wild beasts, and by that means perish, God bid him not to entertain such a melancholy suspicion, and to go over all the earth without fear of what mischief he might suffer from wild beasts; and setting a mark upon him that he might be known, he commanded him to depart.

And when Cain had travelled over many countries, he, with his wife, built a city, named Nod, which is a place so called, and there he settled his abode, where also he had children. However, he did not accept of his punishment in order to amendment, but to increase his wickedness; for he only aimed to procure everything that was for his own bodily pleasure, though it obliged him to be injurious to his neighbors. He augmented his household substance with much wealth, by rapine and violence; he excited his acquaintances to procure pleasures and spoils by robbery, and became a great leader of men into wicked courses. He also introduced a change in that way of simplicity wherein men lived before; and was the author of measures and weights. And whereas they lived innocently and generously while they knew nothing of such arts, he changed the world into cunning craftiness. He first of all set boundaries about lands; he built a city and fortified it with walls, and he compelled his family to come together to it; and called that city Enoch, after the name of his eldest son Enoch. Now Jared was the son of Enoch; whose son was Malaleel; whose son was Methuselah; whose son was Lamech; who had seventy-seven children by two wives, Silla and Ada. Of those children by Ada, one was Jabal; he erected tents and loved the life of a shepherd. But Jubal, who was born of the same mother with him, exercised himself in music; and invented the psaltery and the harp. But Tubal, one of his children by the other wife, exceeded all men in strength, and was very expert and famous in martial performances. He procured what tended to the pleasures of the body by that method; and first of all invented the art of making brass. Lamech was also the father of a daughter, whose name was Naamah; and because he was so skillful in matters of divine revelation, that he knew he was to be punished for Cain's murder of his brother, he made that known to his wives. Nay, even while Adam was alive, it came to pass that the posterity of Cain became exceedingly wicked, everyone successively dying one after another, more wicked than the former. They were intolerable in war, and vehement in robberies; and if anyone were slow to murder people, yet was he bold in his profligate behavior, in acting unjustly and doing injury for gain.

Now, Adam, who was the first man, and made out of the earth (for our discourse must now be about him), after Abel was slain, and Cain fled away on account of his murder, was solicitous for posterity, and had a vehement desire of children, he being two hundred and thirty years old; after which time he lived another seven hundred, and then died. He had indeed many other children, but Seth in particular. As for the rest, it would be tedious to name them; I will, therefore, only endeavor to give an account of those that proceeded from Seth. Now this Seth, when he was brought up, and came to those years in which he could discern what was good, became a virtuous man; and as he was himself of an excellent character, so did he leave children behind him who imitated his virtues. All those proved to be of good dispositions. They also inhabited the same country without dissention, and in a happy condition, without any misfortunes falling upon them, till they died. They also were the inventors of that peculiar sort of wisdom which is concerned with the heavenly bodies and their order. And that their inventions might not be lost before they were sufficiently known, upon Adam's prediction that the world was to be destroyed at one time by the force of fire, and at another time by the violence and quantity of water, they made two pillars; the one of brick, the other of stone; they inscribed their discoveries on them both, that in case the pillar of brick should be destroyed by the flood, the pillar of stone might remain and exhibit those discoveries to mankind; and also inform them that there was another pillar of brick erected by them. Now this remains in the land of Siriad* to this day.

Now this posterity of Seth continued to esteem God as the Lord of the universe, and to have an entire regard to virtue, for seven generations; but in process of time they were perverted, and forsook the practices of their forefathers, and did neither pay those honors to God which were appointed them, nor had they any concern to do justice

---

*Syria?

towards men. But for what degree of zeal they had formerly strewn for virtue, they now showed by their actions a double degree of wickedness, whereby they made God to be their enemy; for many angels of God accompanied with women, and begat sons that proved unjust, and despisers of all that was good, on account of the confidence they had in their own strength, for the tradition is that these men did what resembled the acts of those whom the Grecians call giants. But Noah was very uneasy at what they did; and, being displeased at their conduct, persuaded them to change their dispositions and their acts for the better. But, seeing that they did not yield to him, but were slaves to their wicked pleasures, he was afraid they would kill him, together with his wife and children, and those they had married; so he departed out of that land.

Now God loved this man for his righteousness; yet he not only condemned those other men for their wickedness, but determined to destroy the whole race of mankind, and to make another race that should be pure from wickedness. And cutting short their lives, and making their years not so many as they formerly lived, but one hundred and twenty only, he turned the dry land into sea; and thus were all these men destroyed, but Noah alone was saved."

Having quoted the foregoing description of antediluvian life as recorded in the secular writings of the historian Flavius Josephus, it is illuminating to learn in even greater detail what comes down to us concerning the sinful conditions of Noah's world from a scriptural source—the *Book of Jasher*.

Most of this detail is omitted from Moses' Book of Genesis, but much of it is forcefully, even luridly, described in the *Book of Jasher*, a non-canonical history of the Hebrew people to which the Old Testament (Joshua 10:13 and 2 Samuel 1:18) refers twice, but which, in this author's opinion, is mistakenly assumed to be lost.

Following are excerpts from that work:

"Adam and his wife transgressed the command of God which he commanded them, and God knew it, and his anger was kindled against them and he cursed them.

And the Lord God drove them that day from the Garden of Eden, to till the ground from which they were taken, and they went and dwelt at the east of the Garden of Eden; and Adam knew his wife Eve and she bore two sons and three daughters.

And she called the name of the first born Cain, saying, "I have obtained a man from the Lord," and the name of the other she called Abel, for she said, "In vanity we came into the earth and in vanity we shall be taken from it."

And the boys grew up and their father gave them a possession in the land; and Cain was a tiller of the ground, and Abel a keeper of sheep.

And it was at the expiration of a few years, that they brought an approximating offering to the Lord, and Cain brought from the fruit of the ground, and Abel brought from the firstlings of his flock from the fat thereof, and God turned and inclined to Abel and his offering, and a fire came down from the Lord from heaven and consumed it.

And unto Cain and his offering the Lord did not turn, and he did not incline to it, for he had brought from the inferior fruit of the ground before the Lord, and Cain was jealous against his brother Abel on account of this, and he sought a pretext to slay him.

And in some time after, Cain and Abel, his brother, went one day into the field to do their work; and they were both in the field, Cain tilling and ploughing his ground, and Abel feeding his flock. And the flock passed that part which Cain had ploughed in the ground, and it sorely grieved Cain on this account.

And Cain approached his brother Abel in anger, and he said unto him, "What is there between me and thee that thou comest to dwell and bring thy* flock to feed in my land?"

And Abel answered his brother Cain and said unto him, "What is there between me and thee, that thou shalt eat the flesh of my flock and clothe thyself with their wool?

And now, therefore, put off the wool of my sheep with which thou hast clothed thyself, and recompense me for their fruit and flesh which thou has eaten, and when thou shalt have done this, I will then go from thy land as thou hast said."

And Cain said to his brother Abel, "Surely if I slay thee this day, who will require thy blood from me?"

And Abel answered Cain, saying, "Surely God who has made us in the earth, he will avenge my cause, and he will require my blood from thee shouldst thou slay me, for the Lord is the judge and arbiter, and it is he who will requite man according to his evil, and the wicked man according to the wickedness that he may do upon earth.

---

*Familiar pronouns, used throughout this book, reflect similar usage in the King James
    Bible.

And now, if thou shouldst slay me here, surely God knoweth thy secret views, and will judge thee for the evil which thou didst declare to do unto me this day."

And when Cain heard the words which Abel his brother had spoken, behold the anger of Cain was kindled against his brother Abel for declaring this thing.

And Cain hastened and rose up, and took the iron part of his ploughing instrument, with which he suddenly smote his brother and he slew him, and Cain spilt the blood of his brother Abel upon the earth, and the blood of Abel streamed upon the earth before the flock.

And after this, Cain repented having slain his brother, and he was sadly grieved and he wept over him and it vexed him exceedingly.

And Cain rose up and dug a hole in the field, wherein he put his brother's body, and he turned the dust over it.

And the Lord knew what Cain had done to his brother, and the Lord appeared to Cain and said unto him, "Where is Abel thy brother that was with thee?"

And Cain dissembled, and said, "I do not know; am I my brother's keeper?" And the Lord said unto him, "What hast thou done? The voice of thy brother's blood crieth unto me from the ground where thou hast slain him.

For thou hast slain thy brother and hast dissembled before me, and didst imagine in thy heart that I saw thee not, nor knew all thy actions.

But thou didst this thing and didst slay thy brother for naught and because he spoke rightly to thee, and now, therefore, cursed be thou from the ground which opened its mouth to receive thy brother's blood from thy hand, and wherein thou didst bury him.

And it shall be when thou shalt till it, it shall no more give thee its strength as in the beginning, for thorns and thistles shall the ground produce, and thou shalt be moving and wandering in the earth* until the day of thy death."

And at that time Cain went out from the presence of the Lord from the place where he was, and he went moving and** wandering in the land towards the east of Eden, he and all belonging to him.

---

*Although we find that God gave him rest, it might only have been a temporary rest; and as we are neither told in scripture nor in this book anything more relating to Cain, we cannot infer anything contrary to this declaration.

**There is no mention made of the land of Nod: the word here used is נד the participle present of the verb נוד to wander; the last letter of those verbs whose two final letters are similar, is sometimes dropped, and it might have been נדד with on daleth, like the word used in scripture נד without the vau, which is frequently omitted.

And Cain knew his wife in those days, and she conceived and bare a son, and he called his name Enoch, saying in that time the Lord began to give him rest and quiet in the earth.

And at that time Cain also began to build a city; and he built the city and he called the name of the city Enoch, according to the name of his son; for in those days the Lord had given him rest upon the earth, and he did not move about and wander as in the beginning.

And it was in the hundred and thirtieth year of the life of Adam* upon the earth, that he again knew Eve his wife, and she conceived and bare a son in his likeness and in his image, and she called his name Seth**, saying, "Because God has appointed me another seed in the place of Abel, for Cain has slain him."

And Seth lived one hundred and five years, and he begat a son; and Seth called the name of his son Enosh***, saying because in that time the sons of men began to multiply, and to afflict their souls and hearts by transgressing and rebelling against God.

And it was in the days of Enosh that the sons of men continued to rebel and transgress against God, to increase the anger of the Lord against the sons of men.

And the sons of men went and they served other gods, and they forgot the Lord who had created them in the earth; and in those days the sons of men made images of brass and iron, wood and stone, and they bowed down and served them.

And every man made his god and they bowed down to them, and the sons of men forsook the Lord all the days of Enosh and his children; and the anger of the Lord was kindled on account of their works and abominations which they did in the earth.

And the Lord caused the waters of the river Gihon to overwhelm them, and he destroyed and consumed them, and he destroyed the third part of the earth; and notwithstanding this, the sons of men did not turn from their evil ways, and their hands were yet extended to do evil in the sight of the Lord.

And in those days there was neither sowing nor reaping in the earth; and there was no food for the sons of men and the famine was very great in those days.

And the seed which they sowed in those days in the ground became thorns, thistles and briers; for from the days of Adam was this declaration concerning the earth, of the curse of God, which he cursed the earth on account of the sin which Adam sinned before the Lord.

*This agrees with Genesis 5:3
**Seth—"compensation" in Hebrew
***Enos(h)—"mortal" in Hebrew

And it was when men continued to rebel and transgress against God and to corrupt their ways that the earth also became corrupt.

And Enosh lived ninety years and he begat Cainan; and Cainan grew up and he was forty years old, and he became wise and had knowledge and skill in all wisdom, and he reigned over all the sons of men, and he led the sons of men to wisdom and knowledge; for Cainan was a very wise man and had understanding in all wisdom, and with his wisdom he ruled over spirits and demons.

And Cainan knew by his wisdom that God would destroy the sons of men for having sinned upon earth, and that the Lord would in the latter days bring upon them the waters of the flood.

And in those days Cainan wrote upon tablets of stone what was to take place in time to come, and he put them in his treasures.

And Cainan reigned over the whole earth, and he turned some of the sons of men to the service of God.

And when Cainan was seventy years old, he begat three sons and two daughters.

And these are the names of the children of Cainan; the name of the first born Mahlallel, the second Enan, and the third Mered, and their sisters were Adah and Zillah; these are the five children of Cainan that were born to him.

And Lamech, the son of Methusael, became related to Cainan by marriage, and he took his two daughters for his wives, and Adah conceived and bare a son to Lamech, and she called his name Jabal.

And she again conceived and bare a son, and called his name Jubal; and Zillah, her sister, was barren in those days and had no offspring.

For in those days the sons of men began to trespass against God and to transgress the commandments which he had commanded to Adam, to be fruitful and multiply in the earth.

And some of the sons of men caused their wives to drink a draught that would render them barren, in order that they might retain their figures and whereby their beautiful appearance might not fade.

And when the sons of men caused some of their wives to drink, Zillah drank with them.

And the childbearing women appeared abominable in the sight of their husbands, as widows, whilst their husbands lived, for to the barren ones only they were attached.

And in the end of days and years, when Zillah became old,* the Lord opened her womb.

And she conceived and bare a son and she called his name Tubal Cain, saying, "After I had withered away have I obtained him from the Almighty God."

And she conceived again and bare a daughter, and she called her name Naamah, for she said, "After I had withered away have I obtained pleasure and delight."

And Lamech was old and advanced in years, and his eyes were dim that he could not see, and Tubal Cain, his son, was leading him, and it was one day that Lamech went into the field and Tubal Cain his son was with him, and whilst they were walking in the field, Cain, the son of Adam, advanced towards them; for Lamech was very old and could not see much, and Tubal Cain, his son, was very young.

And Tubal Cain told his father to draw his bow, and with the arrows he smote Cain, who was yet far off, and he slew him, <u>for he appeared to them to be an animal.</u>

And the arrows entered Cain's body although he was distant from them, and he fell to the ground and died.

And the Lord requited Cain's evil according to his wickedness, which he had done to his brother Abel, according to the word of the Lord which he had spoken.

And it came to pass when Cain had died, that Lamech and Tubal went to see the animal which they had slain, and they saw, and behold Cain, their grandfather, was fallen dead upon the earth.

And Lamech was very much grieved at having done this, and in clapping his hands together he struck his son and caused his death.

And the wives of Lamech heard what Lamech had done, and they sought to kill him.

And the wives of Lamech hated him from that day, because he slew Cain and Tubal Cain, and the wives of Lamech separated from him, and would not hearken to him in those days.

And Lamech came to his wives, and he pressed them to listen to him about this matter.

And he said to his wives, Adah and Zillah, "Hear my voice, O wives of Lamech, attend to my words, for now you have imagined and said that I slew a man with my wounds, and a child with my stripes for their <u>having done no</u> violence, but surely know that I am old and gray-headed,

---

*It cannot be supposed that they gave Zillah the drink to cause barrenness when she became old, for as it is expressed earlier, it was given to those to retain their figures and whereby their beautiful appearance might not fade.

and that my eyes are heavy through age, and I did this thing unknowingly."

And the wives of Lamech listened to him in this matter, and they returned to him with the advice of their father, Adam, but they bore no children to him from that time, knowing that God's anger was increasing in those days against the sons of men, to destroy them with the waters of the flood for their evil doings.

And Mahlallel, the son of Cainan, lived sixty-five years and he begat Jered; and Jered lived sixty-two years and he begat Enoch.

And all the days that Enoch lived upon the earth were three hundred and sixty-five years.

And when Enoch had ascended into heaven, all the kings of the earth rose and took Methuselah, his son, and anointed him, and they caused him to reign over them in the place of his father.

And Methuselah acted uprightly in the sight of God, as his father Enoch had taught him, and he likewise, during the whole of his life, taught the sons of men wisdom, knowledge and the fear of God, and he did not turn from the good way either to the right or to the left.

But in the latter days of Methuselah the sons of men turned from the Lord. They corrupted the earth, they robbed and plundered each other, and they rebelled against God, and they transgressed, and they corrupted their ways, and would not hearken to the voice of Methuselah, but rebelled against him.

And the Lord was exceedingly wroth against them, and the Lord continued to destroy the seed in those days, so that there was neither sowing nor reaping in the earth.

And still the sons of men did not turn from their evil ways, and their hands were still extended to do evil in the sight of God. And they provoked the Lord with their evil ways, and the Lord was very wroth, and repented that he had made man.

And he thought to destroy and annihilate them and he did so.

And Lamech was one hundred and eighty years old when he took Ashmna, the daughter of Elishaa, the son of Enoch, his uncle, and she conceived.

And at that time the sons of men sowed the ground and a little food was produced, yet the sons of men did not turn from their evil ways, and they trespassed and rebelled against God.

And the wife of Lamech conceived and bare him a son at that time, at the revolution of the year.

And Methuselah called his name Noah*, saying "The earth was in his days at rest and free from corruption", and Lamech his father called his name Menachem**, saying, "This one shall comfort us in our works and miserable toil in the earth, which God has cursed."

And the child grew up and was weaned, and he went in the ways of his father Methuselah, perfect and upright with God.

And all the sons of men departed from the ways of the Lord in those days as they multiplied upon the face of the earth with sons and daughters, and they taught one another their evil practices. And they continued sinning against the Lord.

And every man made unto himself a god. And they robbed and plundered every man, his neighbor, as well as his relative, and they corrupted the earth. And the earth was filled with violence.

And their judges and rulers went to the daughters of men and took their wives by force from their husbands, according to their choice. And the sons of men in those days took from the cattle of the earth, the beasts of the field and the fowl of the air, and taught the mixture of animals of one species with the other in order therewith to provoke the Lord; and God saw the whole earth and it was corrupt for all flesh had corrupted its ways upon earth, all men and all animals.

And the Lord said, "I will blot out man that I created from the face of the earth, yea, from man to the birds of the air, together with cattle and beasts that are in the field, for I repent that I made them."

And all men who walked in the ways of the Lord died in those days before the Lord brought the evil upon man which he had declared. For this was from the Lord that they should not see the evil which the Lord spoke of concerning the sons of men.

And Noah found grace in the sight of the Lord, and the Lord chose him and his children to raise up seed from them upon the face of the whole earth.

And all who followed the Lord died in those days, before they saw the evil which God declared to do upon earth.

And after the lapse of many years, in the four hundred and eightieth year of the life of Noah, when all those men who followed the Lord had died away from amongst the sons of men, and only Methuselah was then left, God said unto Noah and Methuselah, saying, "Speak ye, and proclaim to the sons of men, saying, 'thus saith the Lord, return from your evil ways and forsake your works, and the Lord will repent of the evil that he declared to do to you, so that it shall not come to pass.'

*Noah–"rest" in Hebrew
**Menachem–"Comforter" in Hebrew

For thus saith the Lord, 'behold I give you a period of one hundred and twenty years; if you will turn to me and forsake your evil ways, then will I also turn away from the evil which I told you, and it shall not exist', saith the Lord."

And Noah and Methuselah spoke all the words of the Lord to the sons of men, day after day, constantly speaking to them.

But the sons of men would not hearken to them, nor incline their ears to their words, and they were stiff-necked.

And the Lord granted them a period of one hundred and twenty years, saying, "If they will return, then will God repent of the evil, so as not to destroy the earth."

And Noah, the son of Lamech, refrained from taking a wife in those days to beget children, for he said, "Surely now God will destroy the earth; wherefore then shall I beget children?"

And Noah was a just man; he was perfect in his generation*, and the Lord chose him to raise up seed from his seed upon the face of the earth.

And the Lord said unto Noah, "Take unto thee a wife and beget children, for I have seen thee righteous before me in this generation.

And thou shalt raise up seed, and thy children with thee, in the midst of the earth"; and Noah went and took a wife, and he chose Naamah, the daughter of Enoch, and she was five hundred and eighty years old.

And Noah was four hundred and ninety-eight years old when he took Naamah for a wife.

And Naamah conceived and bare a son, and he called his name Japheth**, saying, "God has enlarged me in the earth"; and she conceived again and bare a son, and she called his name Shem***, saying, "God has made me a remnant to raise up seed in the midst of the earth."

And Noah was five hundred and two years old when Naamah bare Shem, and the boys grew up and went in the ways of the Lord, in all that Methuselah and Noah, their father, taught them.

And Lamech, the father of Noah, died in those days; yet verily he did not go with all his heart in the ways of his father, and he died in the hundred and ninety-fifth year of the life of Noah.

And all the days of Lamech were seven hundred and seventy years, and he died.

*ancestry
**Japheth—"extender" in Hebrew
***Shem—"renown" in Hebrew

And it was after this that the Lord said to Noah, "The end of all flesh is come before me on account of their evil deeds, and <u>behold I will destroy the earth.</u>

And do thou take unto thee gopher wood, and go to a certain place and make a large ark and place it in that spot.

And thus shalt thou make it; three hundred cubits* its length, fifty cubits broad and thirty cubits high.

And thou shalt make unto thee a door, open at its side, and to a cubit thou shalt finish above, and cover it within and without with pitch.

And behold I will bring the flood of waters upon the earth, and all flesh be destroyed from under the heavens; all that is upon earth shall perish.

And thou and thy household shall go and gather two couple of all living things, male and female, and shall bring them to the ark to raise up seed from them upon earth.

And gather unto thee all food that is eaten by all the animals, that there may be food for thee and for them.

And thou shalt choose for thy sons three maidens from the daughters of men, and they shall be wives to thy sons."

And Noah rose up, and he made the ark in the place where God had commanded him, and Noah did as God had ordered him.

In his five hundred and ninety-fifth year, Noah commenced to make the ark, <u>and he made the ark in five years as the Lord had commanded.</u>

Then Noah took the three daughters of Eliakim, son of Methuselah, for wives for his sons, as the Lord had commanded Noah.

And it was at that time Methuselah, the son of Enoch, died; nine hundred and sixty years old was he at his death.

At that time, after the death of Methuselah, the Lord said to Noah, "Go thou with thy household into the ark; behold I will gather to thee all the animals of the earth, the beasts of the field and the fowls of the air, and they shall all come and surround the ark.

And thou shalt go and seat thyself by the doors of the ark, and all the beasts, the animals, and the fowl shall assemble and place themselves before thee. <u>And such of them as shall come and crouch before thee shalt thou take</u> and deliver into the hands of thy sons, who shall bring them to the ark. <u>And all that will stand before thee, thou shalt leave.</u>"

And the Lord brought this about on the next day, and animals, beasts and fowl came in great multitudes and surrounded the ark.

*sacred cubit—about 25 inches long

And Noah went and seated himself by the door of the ark, and of all flesh that crouched before him, he brought into the ark, and all that stood before him he left upon earth.

And a lioness came with her two whelps, male and female, and the three crouched before Noah. And the two whelps rose up against the lioness and smote her and made her flee from her place, and she went away, and they returned to their places and crouched upon the earth before Noah.

And the lioness ran away and stood in the place of the lions.

And Noah saw this and wondered greatly, and he rose and took the two whelps and brought them into the ark.

And Noah brought into the ark from all living creatures that were upon earth, so that there was none left but which Noah brought into the ark.

Two and two came to Noah into the ark, but from the clean animals, and clean fowls, he brought seven couples, as God had commanded him.

And all the animals, and beasts, and fowl, were still there, and they surrounded the ark at every place, and the rain had not descended till seven days after.

And on that day, the Lord caused the whole earth to shake, and the sun darkened, and the foundations of the world raged, and the whole earth was moved violently, and the lightning flashed, and the thunder roared, and all the fountains in the earth were broken up, such as was not known to the inhabitants before; and God did this mighty act in order to terrify the sons of men that there might be no more evil upon earth.

And still the sons of men would not return from their evil ways, and they increased the anger of the Lord at that time, and did not even direct their hearts to all this.

And at the end of seven days, in the six-hundredth year of the life of Noah, the waters of the flood were upon the earth.

And all the fountains of the deep were broken up, and the windows of heaven were opened, and the rain was upon the earth forty days and forty nights.

And Noah and his household, and all the living creatures that were with him, came into the ark on account of the waters of the flood, and the Lord shut him in.

And all the sons of men that were left upon the earth became exhausted through evil on account of the rain, for the waters were coming more violently upon the earth, and the animals and beasts were still surrounding the ark.

And the sons of men assembled together, <u>about seven hundred thousand men and women</u>, and they came unto Noah to the ark.

And they called to Noah, saying, "<u>Open for us that we may come to thee in the ark—and wherefore shall we die?</u>"

And Noah, with a loud voice, answered them from the ark, saying, "<u>Have you not all rebelled against the Lord and said that he does not exist? And, therefore, the Lord brought upon you this evil</u>, to destroy and cut you off from the face of the earth.

Is not this the thing that I spoke to you of one hundred and twenty years back, and you would not hearken to the voice of the Lord, and now do you desire to live upon earth?"

And they said to Noah, "We are ready to return to the Lord; only open for us that we may live and not die."

And Noah answered them, saying, "Behold now that you see the trouble of your souls, you wish to return to the Lord; why did you not return during these hundred and twenty years which the Lord granted you as the determined period?

But now you come and tell me this on account of the troubles of your souls,<u> now also the Lord will not listen to you</u>, neither will he give ear to you on this day, so that you will not now succeed in your wishes."

And the sons of men approached in order to break into the ark, to come in on account of the rain, for they could not bear the rain upon them.

And the Lord sent all the beasts and animals that stood round the ark. <u>And the beasts overpowered them and drove them from that place</u>, and every man went his way and scattered themselves upon the face of the earth.*

Finis

---

* The Flood occurred in 2344 B.C. While it destroyed the Adamic world, it was not a total, world-wide deluge, as several ancient scriptures affirm and as secular history also confirms.

PART TWO

The Wicked
World of
Lot

*Why God Destroyed
Sodom and Gommorrah*

Prologue

The Book of Genesis provides Bible readers with the names of the descendants of the righteous Shem, second son of Noah, down through ten generations (including Terah) to Nahor, father of Abram.

It touches briefly on Abram's marriage to Sarai, his obedience to God's command to leave Ur of the Chaldees, his sojourn first at Haran and later at Schechem in Canaan, and his trip to Egypt to escape a severe famine. In the course of time, he received this blessing from God:

"I will make of you a great nation, and I will bless you and make your name great, so that you will be a blessing. I will bless those who bless you, and him who curses you I will curse, and by you all the families of the earth shall be blessed."

Abram was also told that God would give the land of Canaan to his descendants. On his journeys he was accompanied by his nephew Lot, son of Abram's half-brother Haran, who died in the fiery furnace prepared by Nimrod in Casdim (Chaldea), from which Abram miraculously escaped.

Upon returning from Egypt, where Pharaoh had showered him with great wealth, Abram journeyed north via the Negeb to Bethel where he parted company with Lot. This is the story of Lot in Sodom, a city so wicked that only he and his two daughters survived God's punishment.

The Fate of Lot

After Abram and his family, including his nephew Lot, had emigrated from Haran to the land of Canaan, each became so wealthy that their servants began to quarrel. The Bible tells us that Abram offered Lot his choice of areas in which to live and pasture his herds and flocks. Lot chose the (then) well-watered Jordan Valley and "moved his tent as far as Sodom," although "the men of Sodom were wicked, (and) great sinners against the Lord." Later, after the victorious battle waged by Amraphel (Nimrod), king of Shinar, and his three fellow kings against the five Canaanite kings of the Jordan Valley, Lot, with all his possessions, was seized by Nimrod and taken captive. Abram, his uncle, came quickly to his rescue, and Lot was soon restored to his former estate. Later still, the Lord said to Abram, "Because the outcry against Sodom and Gomorrah is great, and their sin is very grave, I will go down to see whether they have done altogether according to the outcry which has come to me; and if not, I will know."

Abram then did his best to dissuade the Lord from His announced intent to destroy the city. He obtained the Lord's agreement not to do so if as few as ten righteous people could be found there*. Unfortunately, Lot's two engaged daughters and their intended husbands ignored Lot's urgent plea to them to flee, "'for the Lord is about to destroy the city.' But he seemed to his sons-in-law to be jesting." So matters stood when only Lot, his wife, and his two other virgin daughters were seized by the hand and led to safety by the two angels who had been their guests. Yet Lot's wife never made it all the way out of the city, as she was turned into a pillar of salt for a reason revealed in an ancient scripture, answering a question that has puzzled Bible readers for over three millennia. In the end, Lot and his

---

*If Lot's four daughters, two married and two affianced, and Lot's four sons-in-law, had been found righteous, God promised Abraham that the cities would be spared. They ignored the warning.

two daughters found refuge in the famous cave of Adullam, believing the whole world to have been destroyed. For the consequences of this error, which led to a confused case of misbegotten offspring and incestuous relationships, readers can find the sordid details in Genesis 19:30-38, as well as in the *Book of Jasher.*

With this largely familiar background, it should interest readers to know what really caused God's decision to destroy Sodom and the other four cities of the Jordan Valley, even before the Sodomites' depraved behavior in front of Lot's house (Genesis 19:1-13).

For a description of the egregious sins which so angered God and brought deserved destruction on everything and everyone living in the area, the following explanation from the *Book of Jasher* is immensely revealing:

> In those days, all the people of Sodom and Gomorrah, and of the whole five cities, were exceedingly wicked and sinful against the Lord, and they provoked the Lord with their abominations. And they strengthened in acting abominably and scornfully before the Lord, and their wickedness and crimes were in those days great before the Lord.
>
> And they had in their land a very extensive valley, about half a day's walk, and in it there were fountains of water and a great deal of herbage surrounding the water.
>
> And all the people of Sodom and Gomorrah went there four times in the year, with their wives and children and all belonging to them, and they rejoiced there with timbrels and dances.*
>
> And in the time of rejoicing they would all rise and lay hold of their neighbors' wives, and some, the virgin daughters of their neighbors, and they enjoyed them, and each man saw his wife and daughter in the hands of his neighbor and did not say a word.
>
> And they did so from morning to night, and they afterward returned home each man to his house and each woman to her tent; so they always did four times in the year.
>
> Also when a stranger came into their cities and brought goods which he had purchased with a view to dispose of them, the people of these cities would assemble, men, women and children, young and old, and go to the man and take his goods by force, giving a little to each man until there was an end to all the goods of the owner which he had brought into the land.

---

*An early Woodstock love-in?

And if the owner of the goods quarreled with them, saying, "What is this work which you have done to me?", then they would approach to him one by one, and each would show him the little which he took and taunt him, saying, "I only took that little which thou didst give me"; and when he heard this from them all, he would arise and go from them in sorrow and bitterness of soul, when they would all arise and go after him, and drive him out of the city with great noise and tumult.

And there was a man from the country of Elam who was leisurely going on the road, seated upon his ass, which carried a fine mantle of divers colors, and the mantle was bound with a cord upon the ass.

And the man was on his journey passing through the street of Sodom when the sun set in the evening, and he remained there in order to abide during the night, but no one would let him into his house; and at that time there was in Sodom a wicked and mischievous man, one skillful to do evil, and his name was Hedad.*

And he lifted up his eyes and saw the traveller in the street of the city, and he came to him and said, "Whence comest thou and whither dost thou go?"

And the man said to him, "I am travelling from Hebron to Elam, where I belong, and as I passed the sun set and no one would suffer me to enter his house, though I had bread and water and also straw and provender for my ass, and am short of nothing."

And Hedad answered and said to him, "All that thou shalt want shall be supplied by me, but in the street thou shalt not abide all night."

And Hedad brought him to his house, and he took off the mantle from the ass with the cord, and brought them to his house. And he gave the ass straw and provender whilst the traveller ate and drank in Hedad's house, and he abided there that night.

And in the morning the traveller rose up early to continue his journey, when Hedad said to him, "Wait, comfort thy heart with a morsel of bread and then go", and the man, did so; and he remained with him, and they both ate and drank together during the day when the man rose up to go.

And Hedad said to him, "Behold now the day is declining, thou hadst better remain all night that thy heart may be comforted"; and he pressed him so that he tarried there all night, and on the second day he rose up early to go away, when Hedad pressed him, saying, "Comfort thy heart with a morsel of bread and then go"; and he remained and ate with him also the second day, and then the man rose up to continue his journey.

*a Syrian name

And Hedad said to him, "Behold now the day is declining. Remain with me to comfort thy heart and in the morning rise up early and go thy way."

And the man would not remain, but rose and saddled his ass, and whilst he was saddling his ass the wife of Hedad said to her husband, "Behold this man has remained with us for two days eating and drinking and he has given us nothing, and now shall he go away from us without giving anything?" And Hedad said to her, "Be silent."

And the man saddled his ass to go, and he asked Hedad to give him the cord and mantle to tie it upon the ass.

And Hedad said to him, "What sayest thou?" And he said to him "That thou my lord shalt give me the cord and the mantle made with divers colors which thou didst conceal with thee in thy house to take care of it."

And Hedad answered the man, saying, "This is the interpretation of thy dream, the cord which thou didst see means that thy life will be lengthened out like a cord, and having seen the mantle colored with all sorts of colors means that thou shalt have a vineyard in which thou wilt plant trees of all fruits."

And the traveller answered, saying, "Not so my lord, for I was awake when I gave thee the cord and also a mantle woven with different colors, which thou didst take off the ass to put them by for me." And Hedad answered and said, "Surely I have told thee the interpretation of thy dream and it is a good dream, and this is the interpretation thereof.

Now the sons of men give me four pieces of silver, which is my charge for interpreting dreams, and of thee only I require three pieces of silver."

And the man was provoked at the words of Hedad, and he cried bitterly, and he brought Hedad to Serak, judge of Sodom.

And the man laid his cause before Serak, the judge, when Hedad replied, saying, "It is not so, but thus the matter stands." And the judge said to the traveller, "This man Hedad telleth thee truth, for he is famed in the cities for the accurate interpretation of dreams."

And the man cried at the word of the judge, and he said, "Not so my lord, for it was in the day that I gave him the cord and mantle which was upon the ass, in order to put them by in his house." And they both disputed before the judge, the one saying thus the matter was, and the other declaring otherwise.

And Hedad said to the man, "Give me four pieces of silver that I charge for my interpretations of dreams. I will not make any allowance.

And give me the expense of the four meals that thou didst eat in my house."

And the man said to Hedad, "Truly I will pay thee for what I ate in thy house, only give me the cord and mantle which thou didst conceal in thy house."

And Hedad replied before the judge and said to the man, "Did I not tell thee the interpretation of thy dream? The cord means that thy days shall be prolonged like a cord, and the mantle, that thou wilt have a vineyard in which thou wilt plant all kinds of fruit trees.

This is the proper interpretation of thy dream, now give me the four pieces of silver that I require as a compensation, for I will make thee no allowance."

And the man cried at the words of Hedad and they both quarreled before the judge, and the judge gave orders to his servants, who drove them rashly from the house.

And they went away quarreling from the judge, when the people of Sodom heard them. And they gathered about them and they exclaimed against the stranger, and they drove him rashly from the city.

And the man continued his journey upon his ass with bitterness of soul, lamenting and weeping.

And whilst he was going along, he wept at what had happened to him in the corrupt city of Sodom.

And the cities of Sodom had four judges to four cities, and these were their names, Serak in the city of Sodom, Sharkad in Gomorrah, Zabnac in Admah, and Menon in Zeboyim.

And Eliezer, Abraham's servant, applied to them different names, and he converted Serak to Shakra, Sharkad to Shakrura, Zabnac to Kezobim, and Menon to Matzlodin.

And by desire of their four judges, the people of Sodom and Gomorrah had beds erected in the streets of the cities. And if a man came to these places, they laid hold of him and brought him to one of their beds, and by force made him lie in them.

And as he lay down, three men would stand at his head and three at his feet and measure him by the length of the bed, and if the man was less than the bed, these six men would stretch him at each end, and when he cried out to them they would not answer him.

And if he was longer than the bed, then they would draw together the two sides of the bed at each end until the man had reached the gates of death.

And if he continued to cry out to them, they would answer him, saying, "Thus shall it be done to a man that cometh into our land."

And when men heard all these things that the people of the cities of Sodom did, they refrained from coming there.

And when a poor man came to their land, they would give him silver and gold and cause a proclamation in the whole city not to give him a morsel of bread to eat. And if the stranger should remain there some days and die from hunger, not having been able to obtain a morsel of bread, then at his death all the people of the city would come and take their silver and gold which they had given to him.

And those that could recognize the silver or gold which they had given him took it back, and at his death they also stripped him of his garments, and they would fight about them, and he that prevailed over his neighbor took them.

They would after that carry him and bury him under some of the shrubs in the deserts; so they did all the days to anyone that came to them and died in their land.

And in the course of time, Sarah* sent Eliezer to Sodom to see Lot and inquire after his welfare.

And Eliezer went to Sodom, and he met a man of Sodom fighting with a stranger, and the man of Sodom stripped the poor man of all his clothes and went away.

And this poor man cried to Eliezer and supplicated his favor on account of what the man of Sodom had done to him.

And he said to him, "Why dost thou act thus to the poor man who came to thy land?"

And the man of Sodom answered Eliezer, saying, "Is this man thy brother, or have the people of Sodom made thee a judge this day, that thou speakest about this man?"

And Eliezer strove with the man of Sodom on account of the poor man, and when Eliezer approached to recover the poor man's clothes from the man of Sodom, he hastened and with a stone smote Eliezer in the forehead.

And the blood flowed copiously from Eliezer's forehead. And when the man saw the blood, he caught hold of Eliezer, saying, "Give me my hire for having rid thee of this bad blood that was in thy forehead, for such is the custom and the law in our land."

And Eliezer said to him, "Thou hast wounded me and requires me to pay thee thy hire?"; and Eliezer would not hearken to the words of the man of Sodom.

*Wife of Abraham

And the man lay hold of Eliezer and brought him to Shakra, the judge of Sodom, for judgment.

And the man spoke to the judge, saying, "I beseech thee, my lord, thus has this man done, for I smote him with a stone, that the blood flowed from his forehead, and he is unwilling to give me my hire." And the judge said to Eliezer, "This man speaketh truth to thee, give him his hire, for this is the custom in our land"; and Eliezer heard the words of the judge and he lifted up a stone and smote the judge, and the stone struck on his forehead and the blood flowed copiously from the forehead of the judge. And Eliezer said, "If this, then, is the custom in your land, give thou unto this man what I should have given him, for this has been thy decision, thou didst decree it."

And Eliezer left the man of Sodom with the judge, and he went away.

And when the kings of Elam had made war with the kings of Sodom, the kings of Elam captured all the property of Sodom, and they took Lot captive with his property; and when it was told to Abraham, he went and made war with the kings of Elam. And he recovered from their hands all the property of Lot, as well as the property of Sodom.

At that time the wife of Lot bare him a daughter, and he called her name Paltith, saying, "Because God had delivered him and his whole household from the kings of Elam"; and Paltith, daughter of Lot, grew up, and one of the men of Sodom took her for a wife.

And a poor man came into the city to seek a maintenance, and he remained in the city some days. And all the people of Sodom caused a proclamation of their custom not to give this man a morsel of bread to eat until he dropped dead upon the earth, and they did so.

And Paltith, the daughter of Lot, saw this man lying in the streets starved with hunger, and no one would give him anything to keep him alive, and he was just upon the point of death.

And her soul was filled with pity on account of the man, and she fed him secretly with bread for many days. And the soul of this man was revived.

For when she went forth to fetch water, she would put the bread in the water pitcher, and when she came to the place where the poor man was, she took the bread from the pitcher and gave it him to eat; so she did many days.

And all the people of Sodom and Gomorrah wondered how this man could bear starvation for so many days.

And they said to each other, "This can only be that he eats and drinks, for no man can bear starvation for so many days or live as this man has, without even his countenance changing." And three men concealed themselves in a place where the poor man was stationed, to know who it was that brought him bread to eat.

And Paltith, daughter of Lot, went forth that day to fetch water, and she put bread into her pitcher of water, and she went to draw water by the poor man's place. And she took out the bread from the pitcher and gave it to the poor man and he ate it.

And the three men saw what Paltith did to the poor man, and they said to her, "It is thou, then, who hast supported him, and therefore has he not starved, nor changed in appearance, nor died like the rest."

And the three men went out of the place in which they were concealed, and they seized Paltith and the bread which was in the poor man's hand.

And they took Paltith and brought her before their judges, and they said to them, "Thus did she do, and it is she who supplied the poor man with bread, therefore did he not die all this time. Now, therefore, declare to us the punishment due to this woman for having transgressed our law."

And the people of Sodom and Gomorrah assembled and kindled a fire in the street of the city, and they took the woman and cast her into the fire and she was burned to ashes.

And in the city of Admah, there was a woman to whom they did the like.

For a traveller came into the city of Admah to abide there all night with the intention of going home in the morning. And he sat opposite the door of the house of the young woman's father, to remain there, as the sun had set when he had reached that place; and the young woman saw him sitting by the door of the house.

And he asked her for a drink of water, and she said to him, "Who art thou?" And he said to her, "I was this day going on the road and reached here when the sun set, so I will abide here all night, and in the morning I will arise early and continue my journey."

And the young woman went into the house and fetched the man bread and water to eat and drink.

And this affair became known to the people of Admah, and they assembled and brought the young woman before the judges that they should judge her for this act.

And the judge said "The judgment of death must pass upon this woman, because she transgressed our law; and this, therefore, is the decision concerning her."

And the people of those cities assembled and brought out the young woman and anointed her with honey from head to foot, as the judge had decreed. And they placed her before a swarm of bees which were then in their hives, and the bees flew upon her and stung her that her whole body was swelled.

And the young woman cried out on account of the bees, but no one took notice of her or pitied her, and her cries ascended to heaven.

And the Lord was provoked at this and at all the works of the cities of Sodom, for they had abundance of food and had tranquility amongst them, and still would not sustain the poor and the needy. And in those days their evil doings and sins became great before the Lord.

And the Lord sent for two of the angels (that had come to Abraham's house) to destroy Sodom and its cities.

And the angels rose up from the door of Abraham's tent after they had eaten and drunk, and they reached Sodom in the evening. And Lot was then sitting in the gate of Sodom and when he saw them, he rose to meet them and he bowed down to the ground.

And he pressed them greatly and brought them into his house, and he gave them victuals which they ate, and they abided all night in his house.

And the angels said to Lot, "Arise, go forth from this place, thou and all belonging to thee, lest thou be consumed in the iniquity of this city, for the Lord will destroy this place."

And the angels laid hold upon the hand of Lot and upon the hand of his wife, and upon the hands of his children, and all belonging to him, and they brought him forth and set him without the cities.

And they said to Lot, "Escape for thy life"; and he fled and all belonging to him.

Then the Lord rained upon Sodom and upon Gomorrah and upon all these cities brimstone and fire from the Lord out of heaven.

And he overthrew these cities, all the plain and all the inhabitants of the cities, and that which grew upon the ground. And Ado, the wife of Lot, looked back to see the destruction of the cities, for her compassion was moved on account of her daughters who remained in Sodom, for they did not go with her.

And when she looked back, she became a pillar of salt, and it is yet in that place unto this day.

And the oxen which stood in that place daily licked up the salt to the extremities of their feet, and in the morning it would spring forth afresh, and they again licked it up unto this day.

And Lot and two of his daughters that remained with him fled and escaped to the cave of Adullam, and they remained there for some time.

And Abraham rose up early in the morning to see what had been done to the cities of Sodom; and he looked and beheld the smoke of the cities going up like the smoke of a furnace.

And Lot and his two daughters remained in the cave, and they made their father drink wine, and they lay with him, for they said "There was no man upon earth that could raise up seed for them", for they thought that the whole earth was destroyed.

And they both lay with their father, and they conceived and bare sons. And the first born called the name of her son Moab*, saying, "From my father did I conceive him"; he is the father of the Moabites unto this day.

And the younger also called her son Ben-Ami**; he is the father of the children of Ammon unto this day.

And after this, Lot and his two daughters went away from there, and he dwelt on the other side of the Jordan with his two daughters and their sons. And the sons of Lot grew up, and they went and took themselves wives from the land of Canaan, and they begat children and they were fruitful and multiplied.

In the *Book of Jubilees*, there is confirmation of the destruction described earlier, as follows:

In that month, the Lord executed the judgment of Sodom and Gomorrah and Zeboim and all of the district of the Jordan. And he burned them with fire and sulphur and he annihilated them till this day just as (he said), "behold, I have made known to you all of their deeds that (they were) cruel and great sinners and they were polluting themselves and they were fornicating in their flesh and they were causing pollution upon the earth. And thus the Lord will execute judgment like the judgment of Sodom on places where they act according to the pollution of Sodom.

And we saved Lot because the Lord remembered Abraham and he brought him out from the midst of the overthrow. And he and his daughters also committed sins upon the earth which were not (committed) on the earth from the days of Adam until his time, because

*Moab—"water of a father" in Hebrew
**Ben Ammon—"son of a relative" in Hebrew

the man lay with his daughters. And behold it is commanded and it is engraved concerning all of his seed in the heavenly tablets so that he will remove them and uproot them and execute their judgment just like the judgment of Sodom and so that he will not leave seed of man for him on the earth in the day of judgment."

Completing the picture of depravity which prevailed in the four sin cities of the Jordan Valley is the account given in *The Legends of the Jews*, Book One (described under "Sources"). Most of this account repeats, frequently verbatim, the previous narrative from the *Book of Jasher*, but there are certain additions, colorful and explanatory, which deserve to be included in an effort to make the story fully understandable. Here we find why Eliezar, Abraham's servant, chose to alter the names of the various crooked town judges to better suit their true characters. Here, too, is the answer to why Lot's wife, Ado, was turned into salt. It is apparent that Mr. Louis Ginsberg, compiler of *Legends*, must have run a very fine-tooth comb through all his rabbinical sources to come up with these strands of historic golden thread to embellish even Jasher's carefully woven tale.

Herewith are the pertinent additions, omitting the many duplications from previously cited sources:

The inhabitants of Sodom and Gomorrah and the three other cities of the plain were sinful and godless. In their country there was an extensive vale, where they foregathered annually with their wives and their children and all belonging to them to celebrate a feast lasting several days and consisting of the most revolting orgies. If a stranger merchant passed through their territory, he was besieged by them all, big and little alike, and robbed of whatever he possessed. Each one appropriated a bagatelle, until the traveller was stripped bare. If the victim ventured to remonstrate with one or another, he would show him that he had taken a mere trifle, not worth talking about. And the end was that they hounded him from the city.

As Sodom had a judge worthy of itself, so also had the other cities—Sharkar in Gomorrah, Zabnak in Admah, and Manon in Zeboiim. Eliezer, the bondman of Abraham, made slight changes in the names of these judges, in accordance with the nature of what they did: The first he called Shakara, meaning "liar"; the second, Shakrura, meaning "archdeceiver"; the third, Kazban, meaning "falsifier," and the fourth, Mazle-Din, meaning "perverter of judgment."

Once Eliezer, the bondman of Abraham, went to Sodom at the bidding of Sarah to inquire after the welfare of Lot. He happened to enter the city at the moment when the people were robbing a stranger of his garments. Eliezer espoused the cause of the poor wretch, and the Sodomites turned against him; one threw a stone at his forehead and caused considerable loss of blood. Instantly, the assailant, seeing the blood gush forth, demanded payment for having performed the operation of cupping. Eliezer refused to pay for the infliction of a wound upon him, and he was haled before the judge Shakkara. The decision went against him, for the law of the land gave the assailant the right to demand payment. Eliezer quickly picked up a stone and threw it at the judge's forehead. When he saw that the blood was flowing profusely, he said to the judge, "pay my debt to the man and give me the balance."

The cause of their cruelty was their exceeding great wealth. Their soil was gold, and in their miserliness and their greed for more and more gold, they wanted to prevent strangers from enjoying aught of their riches. Accordingly, they flooded the highways with streams of water, so that the roads to their city were obliterated, and none could find the way thither. They were as heartless toward beasts as toward men. They begrudged the birds what they ate, and therefore extirpated them. They behaved impiously toward one another, too, not shrinking back from murder to gain possession of more gold. If they observed that a man owned great riches, two of them would conspire against him. They would beguile him to the vicinity of ruins, and while the one kept him on the spot by pleasant converse, the other would undermine the wall near which he stood, until it suddenly crashed down upon him and killed him. Then the two plotters would divide his wealth between them.

Another method of enriching themselves with the property of others was in vogue among them. They were adroit thieves. When they made up their minds to commit theft, they would first ask their victim to take care of a sum of money for them, which they smeared with strongly scented oil before handing it over to him. The following night, they would break into his house and rob him of his secret treasures, led to the place of concealment by the smell of the oil.

Their laws were calculated to do injury to the poor. The richer a man, the more he was favored before the law. The owner of two oxen was obliged to render one day's shepherd service, but if he had but one ox, he had to give two days' service. A poor orphan, who was thus forced to tend the flocks a longer time than those who were blessed with large herds, killed all the cattle entrusted to him in order to take revenge upon his oppressors, and he insisted, when the skins were assigned, that the owner of two head of cattle should have but one skin, but the owner of one head should receive two skins in correspondence to the method pursued in assigning the work. For the use of the ferry, a traveller had to pay four zuz, but if he waded through the water, he had to pay eight zuz.

The angels left Abraham at noon time, and they reached Sodom at the approach of evening. As a rule, angels proclaim their errand with the swiftness of lightning, but these were angels of mercy, and they hesitated to execute their work of destruction, ever hoping that the evil would be turned aside from Sodom. With nightfall, the fate of Sodom was sealed irrevocably, and the angels arrived there.

Bred in the house of Abraham, Lot had learned from him the beautiful custom of extending hospitality, and when he saw the angels before him in human form, thinking they were wayfarers, he bade them turn aside and tarry all night in his house. But as the entertainment of strangers was forbidden in Sodom on penalty of death, he dared invite them only under cover of the darkness of night, and even then he had to use every manner of precaution, bidding the angels to follow him by devious ways.

The angels, who had accepted Abraham's hospitality without delay, first refused to comply with Lot's request, for it is a rule of good breeding to show reluctance when an ordinary man invites one, but to accept the invitation of a great man at once. Lot, however, was insistent and carried them into his house by main force. At home he had to overcome the opposition of his wife, for she said, "if the inhabitants of Sodom hear of this, they will slay thee."

Lot divided his dwelling in two parts, one for himself and his guests, the other for his wife, so that if aught happened, his wife would be spared. Nevertheless, it was she who betrayed him. She went to a neighbor and borrowed some salt, and to the question whether she could not have supplied herself with salt during daylight hours, she replied, "we had enough salt, until some guests came to us; for them we needed more." In this way the presence of strangers was bruited abroad in the city.

In the beginning, the angels were inclined to hearken to the petition of Lot in behalf of the sinners, but when all the people of the city, big and little, crowded around the house of Lot with the purpose of committing a monstrous crime, the angels warded off his prayers, saying, "hitherto thou couldst intercede for them, but now no longer."

It was not the first time that the inhabitants of Sodom wanted to perpetrate a crime of this sort. They had made a law some time before that all strangers were to be treated in this horrible way. Lot, who was appointed chief judge on the very day of the angels' coming, tried to induce the people to desist from their purpose, saying to them, "my brethren, the generation of the deluge was extirpated in consequence of such sins as you desire to commit. And you would revert to them?" But they replied, "Back! And though Abraham himself came hither, we should have no consideration for him. Is it possible that thou wouldst set aside a law which thy predecessors administered?"

Even Lot's moral sense was no better than it should have been. It is the duty of a man to venture his life for the honor of his wife and his daughters. But Lot was ready to sacrifice the honor of his daughters, wherefore he was punished severely later on.

The angels told Lot who they were and what the mission [was] that had brought them to Sodom, and they charged him to flee from the city with his wife and his four daughters, two of them married, and two betrothed. Lot communicated their bidding to his sons-in-law, and they mocked at him, and said, "O thou fool! Violins, cymbals, and flutes resound in the city, and thou sayest Sodom will be destroyed!" Such scoffing but hastened the execution of the doom of Sodom. The angel Michael laid hold upon the hand of Lot and his wife and his daughters, while with his little finger the angel Gabriel touched the rock whereon the sinful cities were built, and overturned them. At the same time, the rain streaming down upon the two cities was changed into brimstone.

When the angels had brought forth Lot and his family and set them without the city, he bade them run for their lives and not look behind, lest they behold the Shekinah*, which had descended to work the destruction of the cities. The wife of Lot could not control herself. Her mother love made her look behind to see if her married daughters were following. She beheld the Shekinah, and she became a pillar of salt. This pillar exists unto this day. The cattle lick it all day long, and in the evening it seems to have disappeared, but when morning comes it stands there as large as before.

The savior angel had urged Lot himself to take refuge with Abraham. But he refused, and said, "as long as I dwelt apart from Abraham, God compared my deeds with the deeds of my fellow citizens, and among them I appeared as a righteous man. If I should return to Abraham, God will see that his good deeds outweigh mine by far." The angel then granted his plea that Zoar be left undestroyed. This city had

*Shekinah—the cloud of glory

been founded a year later than the other four; it was only fifty-one years old, and therefore the measure of its sins was not so full as the measure of the sins of the neighboring cities.

The destruction of the cities of the plain took place at dawn of the sixteenth day of Nisan, for the reason that there were moon and sun worshippers among the inhabitants. God said, "if I destroy them by day, the moon worshippers will say, 'were the moon here, she would prove herself our savior;' and if I destroy them by night, the sun worshippers will say, 'were the sun here, he would prove himself our savior.' I will, therefore, let their chastisement overtake them on the sixteenth day of Nisan at an hour at which the moon and the sun are both in the skies."

The sinful inhabitants of the cities of the plain not only lost their life in this world, but also their share in the future world. As for the cities themselves, however, they will be restored in the Messianic time.

Finis

Epilogue

The cynics, skeptics and modernists who question and often deny the Biblical account of Sodom's destruction are confronted by several difficulties for which they find it hard to account.

First, there is the present day physical condition of the Dead Sea itself—a lifeless body of water, where once there had been a fertile valley supporting numerous cities, a well watered area where herds, crops, and springs combined to support a considerable Canaanite civilization. Nothing remains of it now but total blight!

Second, we have the prophetic words of Jesus Christ, spoken nearly two thousand years after the event, warning His disciples (Luke 17:26-30), following an earlier warning concerning the days of Noah: "As it was in the days of Noah, so will it be in the days of the Son of Man . . . Likewise, as it was in the days of Lot, they ate, they drank, they bought, they sold, they planted, they built, but on the day when Lot went out from Sodom, fire and sulphur rained from heaven and destroyed them all—so it will be on the day when the Son of Man is revealed."

We have in this prophecy another tie that binds Christian truth with the ancient scriptures, both canonical and non-canonical; the latter simply elaborate on the known and accepted account of the former.

Third, our Lord used the example of Sodom and Gomorrah in comparing their fate with what would happen to certain towns that rejected the Kingdom gospel about to be preached to them by his disciples. In Matthew 10:15, no towns are named, but in Luke 10:12-16 three towns are named.* In Romans 10:27-29, Paul quotes an ominous prediction of Isaiah concerning the distant future made 600 years earlier (Isaiah 1:9-10).

"Though the number of the sons of Israel be as the sand of the sea, only a remnant of them will be saved; for the Lord will execute

* No traces of Chorazin or Capernaum exist today. Bethsaida is a rock strewn ruin.

his sentence upon the earth with vigor and despatch. And as Isaiah predicted, if the Lord of hosts had not left us children, we would have fared like Sodom and been made like Gomorrah."

Strong words indeed, and repeated again by Paul for emphasis! There was to be no timetable by which believers could know beforehand when the Son of man will be revealed. Some readers, however, will be reminded of Jesus' statement (Matthew 16:1-4) to the Pharisees and Sadducees concerning their inability to "interpret the signs of the times to an evil and adulterous generation," except by the sign of Jonah.

The third millennium of the Christian dispensation is only a few months away, as measured by the solar calendar of 365 1/4 days per year (the Jewish record of world events is measured by the lunar calendar, their current year being 5759 years since the creation of Adam). Whether one believes in the immediacy of the fulfillment of our Lord's prophesy or not (and Jesus Christ was indeed a prophet, as described in the first chapter of the Book of Revelation), the prophecy must one day come true. After all, His own statements to His disciples are what present-day believers must rely on without utterly denying Him, and His word of truth.

In the light of such statements, are we not justified in examining the signs of our own time for parallels to Lot's time? One fresh sign of our own time, the atomic age, is barely a half century old. It might seem to be different, until it is compared with God's fire brought down on Sodom nearly four thousand years ago! Maybe this is what is meant by the words of Christ found in Matthew 24:29, that "the powers of the heavens will be shaken" just before the sign of the son of man appears in heaven.

About the Author

Mr. Dudley Foulke Cates has been an avid reader of scriptural history for more than half a century. His early interest in the subject, inspired by his Quaker mother, was partially interrupted by naval service in World War II. It resumed when he began working on Wall Street ("not a case of cause and effect," he says), where he became widely known as an advocate of the then fledgling mutual funds business. In this activity he was credited with a number of important innovations, including pioneering the first money market funds and closed-end bond funds, which helped to popularize that growing industry.

Recently retired to West Palm Beach, Florida, he now has more time to pursue his interest in Biblical history, which had earlier been only a part-time avocation. He professes to be a non-denominational Christian believer, baptized as an Episcopalian (as was his father) at the age of 48. His educational background, at Loomis School, Harvard, and London University, included almost nothing at all of a religious nature. "The blackboard of my familiarity with religion was a total blank," he admits. Only after reading the Bible many times over did he "begin to comprehend" its message, and to appreciate and finally believe its amazingly accurate and truthful explanation of "who we are, why we are here, and where we are going." "This was the missing chalk for the empty blackboard", he realized. He did not himself invent the description of the Holy Bible as "The Owner's operating manual," but he thinks the description is quite accurate. He says that his interest in the non-canonical literature of the ancient past arose from a growing curiosity to learn what the many "lost" scriptures have to tell us about historical events and personages, over and beyond what is revealed in the orthodox, canonical writings with which most Bible readers are somewhat familiar.

While he is new to writing about the esoteric worlds of history and bibliography, he is proud of his descent from a family of writers who made contributions to the advancement of historical knowledge in the late nineteenth century. His maternal grandfather, William Dudley Foulke, was well-known and admired as an historian, biographer, poet, and civil service reformer in the days of Theodore Roosevelt. To his admiring classmates at Columbia University (1869 graduation), Mr. Foulke gave the valedictorian address in ancient Greek, which was apparently understood by everyone present! He went on to become a close friend of Roosevelt, and a member of his "Kitchen Cabinet" (he was T. R.'s successor as Civil Service Commissioner), but his life-long interest was also expressed in such eclectic works as *History of the Langobards* and *Maya*, a romantic novel about early Mayan and Spanish society, following his visit to Yucatan around 1890.

Mr. Cates claims only to have inherited the compelling interest of this far better-educated forebear in these fascinating historical efforts, not his erudition nor his literary talent. He is content to follow in his inquisitive path, as representing a family continuum to be passed along to whichever of his descendants may choose to continue the important work of discovery, which operates just as excitingly backward in unrevealed history as it does forward into the unknown future.

With this book, *Portents of the Coming Millennium*, Mr. Cates continues his contributions to a wider public understanding and appreciation of the non-canonical scriptures. The third installment of a planned series (the first two were *The Rise and Fall of Nimrod* and *Blossoms of the Nile*) this work is intended primarily for those lay readers of the Holy Bible who are curious to know how really depraved the ante-deluvian world had become, and how wicked the people of Sodom and Gomorrah really were before their cities were destroyed by fire and brimstone. It will be followed by a number of other books comprising the "Lamplighter" series of studies garnered from ancient, and largely unknown, historical and scriptural sources.

Principal Sources

Several sources for this book are to be found in *The Old Testament Pseudepigrapha*, an extensive two-volume anthology of non-canonical scriptural works, edited by Professor James H. Charlesworth, Professor of New Testament Language and Literature, Princeton Theological Seminary, Princeton, New Jersey. In his introduction thereto, Professor Charlesworth makes several important comments quoted below:

> "Mere perusal of the Biblical books discloses that their authors depended upon sources that are no longer extant. We know so little about these sources that we cannot be certain of the extent to which they were actual documents.
>
> Some of the documents composed during the early centuries have been transmitted by copyists, many remain lost, and others have been recovered during the last two centuries.
>
> The assumptions that all Christians have the same canon is shattered by the recognition that the Copts and Ethiopians have added other documents to the canon.
>
> It is potentially misleading to use the terms "non-canonical," "canonical," "heresy," and "orthodoxy" when describing either Early Judaism or Early Christianity."

For readers interested in gaining greater understanding of this fascinating subject, there is no more comprehensive source than this work to be found in all of theological literature.

Following are the sources for Portents of the Coming Millennium:

1. *Book of Jasher*– Otherwise described as *"The Book of the Generations of Man Whom God Created Upon Earth on the Day When the Lord God Made Heaven and Earth."*

The book is cited twice in the Old Testament, first in Joshua 10:13 and again in II Samuel 1:18. In both instances, the authors seem to be relying on the Jasher's accounts as authority for their statements, indicating that the Book of Jasher preceded the former as the original source. Although Jasher is assumed by nearly all ecclesiastical authorities to be lost, it can nevertheless be found referenced in eleven notes to the Testament of Judah which is one of the pseudoapocryphal Testaments of the Twelve Patriarchs (three of which have been found at Qumran). These testaments and the aforementioned eleven notes are included in a two-volume work first published in 1913, edited by R. H. Charles, D.D., fellow of Merton College, Oxford, entitled *The Apocrypha and Pseudapocryha of the Old Testament in English* (Oxford Clarendon Press).

The *Book of Jasher* quoted in this anthology was translated about 1835 from a book printed in Venice, circa 1624, from Hebrew into English by an unknown scholar who belonged to the Royal Asiatic Society in London. It was brought to the U.S.A. by one Mordecai Noah in A.D. 1840, then published by M. Noah and Alexander Gould in New York City. The provenance of this work, described in various prefaces thereto, is far more credible than those of almost all other pseudepigraphic scriptures. The fact that it has escaped notice among biblical experts is hard to explain, but the fact of the book's existence is undeniable, especially as it is clearly the source of numerous historical accounts found in *The Legends of the Jews* (L. Ginsberg), although often without identifying attribution. It is also the likely source of some of the legendary material on which Thomas Mann drew in his notable historical novel, *Joseph and his Brothers.*

In the preface to Mordecai Noah's American publication of this work, he quotes the Jewish historian Flavius Josephus as follows:

> "That by this book are to be understood certain records kept in some safe place on purpose, giving an account of what happened among the Hebrews from year to year, and called Jasher, or the "upright," on account of the fidelity of the annals."

2. *Book of Jubilees*, or *"The Account of the Division of the Days of the Law and the Testimony for Annual Observance According to their Weeks (of Years) and their Jubilees Throughout the all the Years of the World,"* just as the Lord told it to Moses on Mount Sinai when he went up to receive the tablets of The Law and The Commandments by the Word of the Lord. "It is sometimes called *"The Little Genesis."* This pseudapocryphal work is included in the two-volume *The Old Testament Pseudepigrapha*, edited by Professor Charlesworth, as previously

described. The text represents a new translation by O. S. Wintermuth, Professor of Religion, Duke University, Durham, North Carolina. From his extensive commentary, we learn that Jubilees was written originally in Hebrew, and not later that 140 B.C. or 152 B.C., by some anonymous "Jew of a priestly family." Professor Wintermuth concedes that the "author used a number of earlier sources. Much of his source material comes from the Ethiopic Bible. *Jubilees* was also found at Qumran. As with similar non-canonical scriptures, it is impossible to identify either the book's origin or the date when it was written."

3. *The Legends of the Jews* by Louis Ginsberg. Translated from his manuscript in German by Henrietta Szold. Originally published in 1909 and re-published in 1960 by the Jewish Publication Society of America (Philadelphia, Pennsylvania).

This compendium of Jewish legends (arranged sequentially, starting with the Creation) is contained in five volumes, plus two volumes of explanatory notes. The author believes he has drawn on most, if not all, of the Rabbinical legends, pseudepigraphical scriptures, and other ancient tales available and known to this renowned scholar, providing us with a parallel account of Biblical history "From Adam to Esther."

In his Preface, he states the following: "Jewish legends can be culled not from the writings of the Synagogue alone; they appear also in those of the Church. Certain Jewish works repudiated by the Synagogue were accepted and mothered by the Church. This is the literature usually denominated apocryphal–pseudepigraphic. From the point of view of legends, the apocryphal books are of subordinate importance, while the pseudepigrapha are fundamental value." Further on he notes: "The pseudepigrapha originated in circles that harbored the germs (sic) from which Christianity developed later on."

In a subsequent preface (to the 1925 edition) he writes: "It is true that Church fathers sometimes sneeringly refer to the 'fabulae judaicae' (Jewish fables), but more often they accept these 'fabulae,' and even refrain from betraying the source from which they drew them." This would appear to make one man's source another man's fable and vice versa!